Dear Reader,

I hope you will keep this book at your desk all through your career. It's not the kind of book you read cover to cover and then put on the shelf.

It is a *survival* guide. Something you can always refer to, read something of value, or just pick up to make you laugh when things get tough. The book does progress from basic tactics to advanced.

I think as you read it you will say to yourself, "I've felt that way or I've had something similar happen to me."

I can visualize all of you out there, sitting behind your desks, managing 101 things. I know the demands of your job and tip my hat to all of you who keep businesses and people going on a day-to-day basis.

It's a jungle out there.

Good luck!

Sincerely,

Joan

THE SURVIVAL GUIDE FOR SECRETARIES AND ADMINISTRATIVE ASSISTANTS

JOAN M. BURGE, CPS

Illustrations by Ginny Petty

HAMPTONROADS
PUBLISHING COMPANY, INC.

Dedication

This book is dedicated to my mother who has always been a beautiful example of womanhood. This one is for you, Mom.

To my father for always being there when I need him and for being an inspiration of courage when things get tough.

To my husband, Dave, for putting up with me through all my job changes and for first giving me the idea for this book.

To my children, Lauren and Brian, for being so patient.

And to all those bosses, who without them, I would not have a story to tell.

Clarification of Terms

Genders used:

The manager's gender in this book is male. When referring to the Survival Tactics, these do not exclude female managers. The secretary's gender although referring to female, does not exclude male secretaries. These genders are used for ease in writing.

The term "secretary": The term secretary is used generically. It refers to any secretary, office manager, or any other related titles.

CONTENTS

INTRODUCTION

Over a twenty-year span, I worked for 12 different companies and 19 different bosses. Why would one individual work for so many different bosses and so many different companies? There are three reasons.

One, because I am the type of person who believes if you aren't happy at what you are doing or where you are doing it, you should move on. Life is too short to be unhappy, especially in a job where you spend most of your waking hours. Think about it: at least 8 hours a day, 5 days a week, 50 weeks a year (2 weeks of vacation), times 35+ years. You deserve to be happy in what you do, not just settle or get by.

The *second* reason for my changes was to better myself, to move to a higher level position or to improve my present status. That is a very good reason for change. Change is good. It forces us to get out of our mundane schedules, to experience new people, places, and work processes. It forces us to grow and helps us deal more effectively with other changes in our life. You should want to grow in your work and personal life. Why would you want to stay the same year after year after year? We only have one life to live. Why not make it the best and fullest possible?

My *third* reason is because I moved to five states over that 20-year span, thus forcing me to leave my jobs. Unfortunately, it always happened at a time when I was working for a really good company, and had a really great boss. These were the jobs that were hard to give up. Really hard to leave. The good news, though, was that as much as I didn't want to leave those organizations, most of the time I ended up in a similar or better situation.

During my working days in the secretarial field, I worked for several Fortune 500 companies as well as small to mid-size businesses in a variety of industries. I use the term secretary to define my positions as: Secretary, Executive Secretary, Administrative Assistant, Marketing Assistant, Guest Services Coordinator, and any other title I was given. I was fortunate to work for some of the finest executives and also for some very difficult bosses!

You can imagine by this time, I have had a broad range of experiences and have been exposed to a multitude of situations. Many of these were educational, frustrating, funny, embarrassing, and very rewarding.

I share with you some true-to-life experiences. I have written each situation to the best of my recollection since some happened quite some time ago. But I can assure you the lesson I learned with each experience has never been forgotten, and I wouldn't have traded one minute of it!

So, let us begin.

1.
WAS THIS IN MY JOB DESCRIPTION?

When I went into the work world, it was so I could learn and grow as an individual as well as contribute to an organization. Contribute I did. Not just in terms of performing secretarial tasks but in many other ways.

No one ever told me I'd have to: sew buttons, cash personal checks, buy birthday gifts for the wife, pack up cases of suntan products, run around town on errands, make fancy coffee, decorate Christmas trees, empty dishwashers, hire limousines, come to work on Saturday and sometimes Sunday, submit medical claims, and know what to do if my boss's child had an asthma attack at school!

SURVIVAL TACTIC #1:

There are many tasks you are asked to perform as a secretary or administrative assistant that are not defined in your written job description. And for each job, each boss, and each company, these undefined duties will vary. There will probably be things you will not necessarily enjoy, but come with the territory. View them as a change from your daily routine, an opportunity to learn something different, and an experience that may help you later in life because you will have had the experience.

2.
IF THAT PHONE RINGS ONE MORE TIME

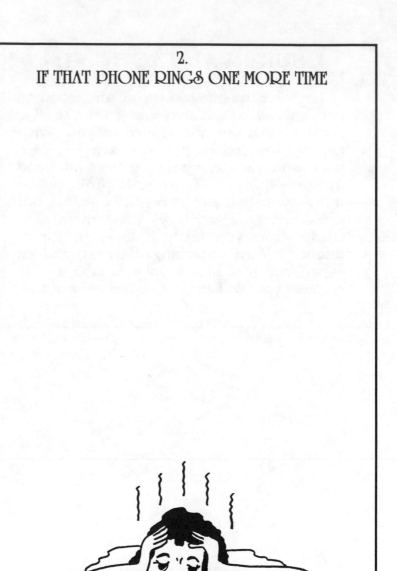

I knew if I ever wanted to leave the secretarial field, I could always apply for a job as a switchboard operator. In over 20 years, I answered the phone approximately 51,000 times.

Did you ever notice how phone calls come in succession? It's not one phone call, and then 20 minutes pass before another. It's more like one call, ring, another call, ring, another call, ring, ring—"Excuse me sir, could you please hold a moment while I answer the other five lines?" And so on.

It never ceased to amaze me that this would occur when I was in a hurry to get something done or the only person picking up calls in the area. And it seemed just at the time when I was ready to pull the plug out of the wall, I'd get a caller who insisted on telling me their life story— even though they could hear other phone lines ringing.

SURVIVAL TACTIC #2:

The best way to handle multiple calls is to be honest with the person on the other end. Honest, but gracious and mannerly. Let them know you need to put them on hold, or you are the only one answering the phones at the present time, or you cannot speak right now. Although you may have to interrupt them to do this, an interruption is better than letting the phones ring, ring, and ring. Nothing is more frustrating to the person calling than having their call unanswered.

You never know who is calling on the other end of the phone. This is the first impression a person gets of you, your boss, and your company. Since this is the first contact, you need to make a good impression. Respond to the call, use a pleasant tone of voice, reflect a positive attitude and eagerness to help.

P.S. This reminds me of a joke I read. The manager asked his new secretary, Miss Smith, "Why don't you ever answer the telephone?" Miss Smith replied, "Why should I? Nine times out of ten, it's for you."

3.
THEY ALL HAVE QUIRKS

Each boss has some little habit or way he likes something done, or something he enjoys on a regular basis, such as with my previous bosses.

* He had to have his teeth cleaned every six months
* He drank a cup of spiced tea every morning as soon as he arrived at the office
* He had to have a glass of cola every afternoon, with ice
* He liked a pitcher of spring water placed on his credenza every morning
* He wanted his daily business paper placed on the left side of his credenza
* He always wanted to know the exact configuration of the plane he was going to fly on
* He loved chocolate!

SURVIVAL TACTIC #3:

Whether or not your manager's little "thing" drives you crazy, it's something you have to be aware of and can use to your benefit. Once you have found what your manager's little quirk is or what special thing he enjoys, or the special way he likes something done, don't wait until you are told to do it or asked to get it.

Learn to anticipate when something is needed and get it done before you are asked. This will win you many "points" with your boss that will be remembered all through the years. Although these may seem trivial and unimportant to you sometimes, they are needs your boss has. If something is a priority on his list, it needs to be a priority on your list.

Remember, it isn't any one big thing that makes a secretary excellent. It's the many little things you do that count.

4.
WHO INVITED YOU TO LUNCH?

With executives involved more and more in meetings, rushing from one to another, discussions are increasingly being held over lunch. It is a good time for everyone to discuss business, get to know each other in a more relaxed atmosphere, and get to eat lunch all at the same time.

The hard part comes when you are coordinating this lovely event for large groups of people. I did this quite frequently in one of my positions where I actually wore three hats in that company: Assistant to the General Manager, Guest Services Coordinator, and Showroom Administrator. In the three years I worked there, I coordinated over 275 lunch meetings. I worked with several caterers in the area who would bring the meals already prepared or would cook in our kitchen.

No big deal, right? Well, it is if you invited only 30 people to lunch, the caterer prepared dishes for 30 people, and 42 showed up to eat!

As this particular group was ushered into the dining area and started to sit down, I began to realize we were quickly running out of seats. The flow of people seemed as if it would never end. It finally did and to my surprise there were 12 people left standing, mouths watering at the sight of the food, wondering if they were going to get to eat or not.

Immediately my boss, another manager, and I started to pull extra tables in from the next room, hurriedly making arrangements for the other guests. That wasn't too difficult. But how was I going to conjure up food for these people?

I went to the kitchen. Thank goodness for the creative caterer I had that day who already had seen what was going on and was making magic out of what little scraps he had left to feed these people. In the meantime, some of our other managers shared what they had on their plates.

It ended up everyone was able to eat. I found out later these additional people had been invited by some of the managers who attended the same meeting, but didn't realize all who attended that meeting were not invited to lunch.

SURVIVAL TACTIC #4:

1) Always clarify in your luncheon invitations or notices, if the majority of people attending are in-house, that the luncheon is catered and only enough lunches will be ordered to serve those invited. This will help prevent any misconceptions by those attending.

2) Always add a few extra lunches to your count when a specific number of plates are being prepared. It's better to have more than not enough. And I'm sure you and the employees in your area will love having something special to eat for a change, if there is extra.

If the meal is being served buffet style, it is not as critical because caterers usually plan for a few extra from the number you give them. But plated meals are not like that.

3) No matter what—look calm and act in control. Don't let others know mass confusion is going on. Be the perfect hostess, managing any last minute disruptions to your perfectly-planned luncheon!

4) Remember to laugh to yourself. No matter how much you plan and how well you plan, people will throw you a curve. Just ride with it.

5.
DO I HAVE TO ORDER MY OWN FLOWERS AGAIN?

Bosses are very busy people and usually do not have time for little things like remembering their secretary's birthday or date of her anniversary with the company.

There are bosses who are also not in tune or familiar with Professional Secretaries Week®and Professional Secretaries Day.® Therefore, it is up to the secretary to educate her boss about this special day and its true meaning. I had one such instance. Well, probably more than one, but this is one I want to share.

This General Manager was as good as they come, but really had no knowledge of Professional Secretaries Day,® probably because his relationship with is previous secretary of six years was not what it should have been.

I had been employed for about four and one-half months when Professional Secretaries Day®rolled around. I graciously explained this event to my boss. I suggested we have a special catered luncheon for the secretaries and their bosses. Our facility was absolutely beautiful. Our industry was manufacturing wood office furniture. Our work areas were of showroom quality. We had a lovely formal dining room, a kitchen three times the size of the one I had at home, and all the goodies that went with it.

I set the dining room table the morning of the luncheon with our good china, crystal, and silver. I had ordered long-stemmed roses with baby's breath for each secretary, in addition to my own flowers. The luncheon was lovely and the secretaries were very appreciative.

Along came the next year—same time—same special event. I once again planned the lunch, sent out invitations, ordered the flowers—plus my own, set up the dining room and so on. And once again it was a success! Well by the third year, I felt it wasn't right to order my own flowers and plan the lunch. After all, this was my day, too.

I decided it was time I had a talk with my manager. He was easy to talk to, receptive, and understood how I felt. He told me when next year came, just tell him the date and the phone numbers of the caterer and florist and he would take care the rest. What a guy!

SURVIVAL TACTIC #5:

Bosses need to be educated. They have so many things on their minds—important things. They do not always pay attention to events that might be important to their assistant. It's not that they don't care nor appreciate them. Many of them haven't been trained in how or what to do.

Take time to express your feelings sincerely and tactfully to your boss. And not just your feelings regarding special events, but also on aspects of your job. Educate your manager so the two of you can build a great working team.

The role of the assistant has changed drastically over the past 20 years. It is predicted that the assistant will see more change, at an accelerated rate, in the next 10 years. Think about it—more changes, in less time, at an accelerated rate. It will be important for you to keep your management staff educated on these changes as they occur.

You can do this in many ways. Verbal communication is always good because the listener can question what they don't understand, ask questions for more detail, and provide immediate feedback.

Other ways of communicating these changes are by sharing articles about the field and upcoming changes, by asking your manager to attend a meeting put on by your professional organization, or creating an in-house newsletter.

17

Communication is the key to educating those around you about your field. As important as being a good sender of information, though, you must also be a good receiver. In other words, listening to your manager's questions and interests about your field so you can help him with your changing role.

P.S. In return, do not forget to acknowledge your boss on Boss's Day! It's in October.

6.
THE RUNAWAY SLIDE SHOW

In today's work world, one almost cannot get by without having to use audio/visual equipment at some point. Depending on the size of your organization, there will be a department or other person responsible for setting up this equipment, or this may be one of your responsibilities.

I held one position in which I was not only the Administrative Assistant to the General Manager, but also wore the hat of Guest Services Coordinator. One of the responsibilities of this position was to learn, maintain, and run a variety of video equipment, single tray slide projectors, and most importantly a nine-tray multi-image slide show. If you have never seen one of these, visualize the following.

A total of nine slide trays set up in three rows, three trays high. In addition, there are two separate operating units. One holds a computerized tape which tells which slide tray should turn when. The other unit contains the voice/music tape that goes along with each slide as it is shown. All fade in and out making a beautiful visual show. All must be set up to perfection and totally in sync for the entire show to work and flow the way it should.

All this equipment was set up in a private room so the audience could not see any of the equipment. I need to explain a little bit of how the room was set up so you can fully appreciate my situation. The viewing audience sat in a viewing room facing the screen. The equipment room was behind the screen. So if a person were to stand up in the equipment room with the lights on in that room, the people in the audience could see that individual.

One day, we had a group of visitors who represented one of our company's biggest vendors. Our Director of Purchasing wanted me to put on the famous nine-tray slide show because it provided insight to our manufacturing facility and talked about our mission of producing quality furniture. The men were all nicely seated in the viewing room while I went into the equipment room to turn on the slide trays and control tapes.

I touched the start button. The first set of three slides came up on the screen vertically, the video tape came on, and the trays began their rotating cycle. All seemed to be working fine so I left the room, went back to my work station, and proceeded to do my work.

It wasn't too long after that the Director of Purchasing appeared at my desk to tell me something went wrong and the slides were no longer in sync with the words. I quickly walked to the video equipment room and opened the door. The room was dark. There I stood in amazement watching nine slide trays going crazy. They each were clicking at different times—one slide would drop down and immediately pop up, and so on. The slides were out of control and did not at all coordinate with what was being said on the voice tape. It was rather funny at first glance, but also embarrassing in view of the prestigious audience viewing this chaos.

The only way to stop the trays from doing what they wanted was to shut everything down, which I did. In case you are wondering what happened to the slide show, I found out the problem was with the programming tape which controlled the entire program.

How did I explain and overcome the runaway slide show to our visitors? Very graciously! I explained to them what had happened and assured them the problem would be taken care of and suggested next time they were in town, they stop in and view the show.

SURVIVAL TACTIC #6:

Be prepared for anything and everything to happen when you work in an office as a secretary or administrative assistant. There will be many instances where things happen beyond your control. The best way to deal with such situations is with grace, poise, professionalism, and honesty.

Crazy things do happen and will happen—just don't fall apart when they do. Most people are very understanding when something occurs that is beyond your control. But their response to such incidences will depend largely on how you respond and deal with the situation.

7.
I HAVE FEELINGS, TOO

I'll never forget the time I worked for the CEO of a financial institution. This was my last job as an executive assistant to a manager—the finale of my 20 years experience in the field.

My desk area was somewhat isolated from a little lobby and entrance to our office suite. On this particular day, I had been extremely busy. Before I realized it, it was 2:30 and I hadn't stopped all day. I thought I would just get a cup of soup from the deli downstairs and take it to my desk so I could continue working.

My boss had just gone into his office when I told him I would be right back. I was going to get some soup. I came back and placed the small soup container to the right side of my computer where it would be hidden in case someone should come into my area. I took the lid off and then walked into my boss's office to hand him some papers. I proceeded to walk out of his office, with him following me only to hear him say, "Don't eat that soup at your desk out in public." He continued to walk away and went out the door from our suite. This was not said with a smile or in jest or even in a mild tone of voice.

I was hurt. I was also upset because he made me feel stupid. I certainly had enough etiquette sense that I was going to be discreet about when and how I ate the soup. I felt like a child being scolded. I took my soup down the hall to a private office, sulked for awhile, and then went back to work.

I logically was able to talk myself into the fact that no one was going to ruin the good day I was having, even if he was a "CEO." And it was up to me to brush it off and go on with the rest of my day, and not hold it against him.

SURVIVAL TACTIC #7:

Eggs and Attitudes.™ They have a lot in common. Imagine in your mind an egg that has not been cooked. It is very fragile. It can easily be broken, boiled, broiled, fried, scrambled, or cracked. Kind of like your attitude. Your attitude is fragile. If you do not guard your attitude, someone is sure to try and take it, fry it, or break it.

Your attitude can greatly affect your work and productivity. If you are too busy feeling hurt, mad, or put down, you cannot do your job. There will always be people doing or saying things to upset you. You will always be faced with situations in the work world that can alter your upbeat attitude. But you have ultimate control as to how you respond. You have a choice. You can decide the course of your attitude.

So, be sure to guard your egg.

8

FOR YOUR EYES ONLY

With almost every job comes the need for a certain degree of confidentiality. At one of the companies I worked, the employees received a quarterly bonus. The percent of bonus was based on the division's profit for that quarter, so it would vary each time. Every quarter an All Employee Meeting was held to review our strengths and weaknesses over that period. It was a major event and one that all employees looked forward to.

The day before the All Employee Meeting was held, there was a management meeting at which my boss, the General Manager of the Division, announced the bonus. About two days before this meeting, my manager would prepare a letter stating how the quarter went and, at the very end, announce the bonus percentage. Now, as most bosses seem to do, mine would have several revisions before the final letter was printed and prepared for handout. This percentage was a "big secret" which was not to be revealed prior to the management meeting. My boss, our Company Controller, and myself were the first ones to know that number.

One unfortunate thing about computers is that the terminals can be seen by anyone standing near or around you. I learned to be very quick with the "switch" key and secretive during my times of revisions. It was incredible how many employees would stop by and see me this time every quarter—sort of stretching their necks to see if they could get a glimpse of the magic number. (Which sometimes was very high.) I would have to laugh to myself because they were so obvious as to why they really came to see me. You probably guessed by now, I learned not to type in the number until the final copy was ready to go.

It was also ironic how people would try to verbally get information from me as to how good (or bad) the quarter was. They would even quote what they thought the percentage would be, hoping I would respond one way or another—with a smile, frown or somehow give myself away with a facial expression. I always held my ground and showed absolutely no expression on my face that would give it away.

SURVIVAL TACTIC #8:

In working with a manager, you see and are told many things which should be held in confidence. It is critical that you maintain those confidences and share them with no one. First, because your boss has confided in you thus proving he trusts you. When a boss realizes he can trust his assistant, he will then divulge other information. Why is this important? Because it allows the assistant to know what is going on in her department and organization. She is on the inside track. If she can be on that track, she will be a major asset to her manager.

Second, revealing information leads to further gossip. And depending on what kind of information is told, can lead to panic within a company. As most rumors go, stories usually get changed as they are passed along the grapevine.

9.
OUT OF THE OFFICE DOESN'T MEAN WHAT IT USED TO

I remember the good old days when a boss would tell me he was going to be out of the office for the day due to outside meetings or customer calls. I would think how wonderful. A day for me to catch up on all those little things I never have time to do when he is in the office.

Not anymore. Thanks to the invention of the car phone. Now when a boss says he is going to be out, if he has a car phone, look out! Because he will call you five or six times a day with a list of at least three or more things to do each time he calls. Please, dear bosses, give those assistants a break!

SURVIVAL TACTIC #9:

Be prepared to relate phone and other messages to your boss. Keep these close at hand, possibly in a special folder near the phone, so when he does call, you can efficiently relate his messages. You may even want to set up a telephone message log on your computer.

Air time is expensive so don't waste it by fumbling for messages and a pen and paper. Keep other pertinent information for discussion with him close at hand. Create a "to discuss" file. Anytime something comes up you need to talk to your manager about, toss it in that file, placing the most critical items on top.

This folder or one similar can also be used even on a daily basis when your boss is in the office. Again, accumulate discussion items in this folder throughout the day that do not have to be addressed immediately. Then either at the end of each day or first thing the next morning, review those items with your manager. This prevents you from interrupting him several times during the day with items that really can wait. Again, assign priorities to these items within the folder so if your manager has to cut your meeting together short, you are at least getting the important things out of the way first.

10

LIFE'S LITTLE EMERGENCIES

Over 50 percent of women in the work force today are mothers. Work in itself is challenging and stressful. But being a working mother creates a whole new list of challenges and stresses to deal with.

It seems just when you are at the most critical point in your work day, you get a call from the school or day care telling you your child is sick, has a fever, fell in the playground, got into a fight, or broke a wire on his brace. Being a working mother myself who went back to work six weeks after each child was born, I experienced several such events.

The scenario usually went like this. I'm at work, covered up with major projects, my boss depending on me to get a list of things done, phones ringing, people requesting everything imaginable, and visitors soon to arrive.

Ring. . . ring. . . "Hello, Mrs. Burge? This is the school calling. Your son threw up on the bus this morning. I have him here with me and we need you to pick him up." I would sit at my desk thinking to myself, "No. Please not today. What will I do? What arrangements can I make?"

SURVIVAL TACTIC #10:

Any working mother at some time is faced with this situation. I think if you are like most working mothers, you do not have the luxury of a live-in nanny. Hopefully, you may have a family member in town that can pick up your child and take care of him/her. Or maybe your spouse's job is such that he can help out. But if you do not have others to help and you are the sole responsible party, then you have a decision to make—and not an easy one if you are in a demanding position or if you are a very conscientious individual and worry about your work getting done.

I was one who did not have any family living in the near vicinity—not even in the same state for that matter. The few close friends I did have, worked. So what did I do?

First I talked to my children to feel them out as to how "sick" they really were. Sometimes children are not really sick, sick. They just don't feel well as the result of getting to bed too late, are nervous about a test, didn't finish their homework, or have been made fun of by other children on the bus or in the school yard. I could tell by listening to my children if they were ill and needed to be picked up or if they were able to make it through the day. Hopefully, you are able to identify this in your child.

Once I decided they were not as bad as

they thought (maybe just complained of a tummy ache or their head hurt), I would tell them I was very sorry but I cannot leave the office and would explain the reasons why. I would tell them I would see them as soon as I could and I loved them.

Once they realized mom was not going to get them, it was amazing how the tone of their voice changed. They sounded better! And many times, by the time they got home, they had even forgotten about feeling ill.

This may sound cold, but a true professional working woman cannot just pick up and leave the office every time she gets a phone call for a sniffle or tiff in the school yard. It is important that your children realize this so they will not make you feel guilty.

The other plan of action is for when your child truly is ill and has to be picked up. First, decide if you really can leave your projects or other priorities at work and get your child yourself. Sometimes this just isn't possible. If you cannot leave, see if your husband, family member, close friend, or sitter can help.

If you must leave the office, make arrangements for those things which must be handled that day to be taken care of by someone else in the office. Explain your situation to your boss and immediate coworkers. If you have other secretaries in your department, pinpoint what absolutely must be done that day and filter the work out to others, requesting their help . Let your boss know what will be taken care of. Let your office know you can be contacted at home if they have questions needing immediate attention.

Much of your response will depend on the type of organization and type of boss you work for. Some are much more understanding of home life situations than others. Only you will be able to judge. But I don't think there is any organization that appreciates their employees consistently having to leave work to take care of home matters.

By handling these situations in a professional manner, you are showing your boss that you take your work seriously and you are concerned that his needs are taken care of. It is especially important to take care of your children's situations responsibly if you are planning to move up within your organization or move into a management position.

Over the years, I encountered people I would classify as somewhat difficult—obnoxious and snobby is more like it—to work with. However, I never encountered one such as this particular product manager of a large company. She really thought she was something and thought secretaries were peons and much beneath her.

She seemed to have a real chip on her shoulder and was on an ego trip. I had not been with this company very long. But it didn't take long to figure this individual out. She consistently talked in a "put down" fashion. She reported to my two bosses so I had much occasion for interaction with her. I tried hard not to let her mannerisms get the best of me and maintained a professional manner when dealing with her. But she didn't seem to get the message.

Finally, I talked to her Senior Manager (one of my bosses). I'll never forget the first words that came out of the manager's mouth. She said "just smack her. You have my permission next time she acts up to smack her." In all my working career, I had never heard management take this perspective on handling difficult people. I am sure my manager was saying it in jest. It was tempting advice. However, I had always been told and have tried to practice being tactful and maintain calmness. Certainly not get violent. Of course, I did not follow this line of advice. I continued to hold my ground and deal with this individual in a professional manner, not allowing myself to be lowered to her level.

SURVIVAL TACTIC #11:

You should never lower your standards or behavior to the level of others, but should definitely strive to maintain a level of professionalism and rise above a situation. The best course to follow when dealing with difficult people is to:

1) Stay calm. You've heard of some of these techniques—counting to ten, taking deep breaths, breaking away from the situation if at all possible, and so on. These techniques may sound funny, but they do work. You need to do something just to break you away from the "heat of the moment."

2) Use your mind; avoid what your immediate emotion tells you to do. It's so easy to use your emotion—to react. Instead, think out the situation. Use your brain. This allows you to be in control—allows you to act as a professional.

3) Attack the problem and not the person. Nothing is solved by verbally attacking the person. It usually only makes things worse. Stay focused on what the problem is—define the real issue that is causing the conflict and think of the consequences if you take a particular action.

4) Act confidently once you have decided how to respond and be responsible for the consequences of your decision. Everything you do or say affects something or someone. You need to see the next step. You need to see beyond just the action you are taking and what

41

happens as a result of your action. It may come back to haunt you.

12.
NOW THIS IS FLYING

Every once and awhile a secretary is afforded some luxuries during her career. I was fortunate enough to experience such things as chocolates from Switzerland, pottery from Spain, silk scarves from Japan, ornaments from Brazil, and the opportunity to travel to some interesting places.

However, one of my favorite experiences was flying on a corporate jet. This was a special privilege as just not any employee could travel on it. This particular company had two corporate jets with eight full-time pilots. The jets were primarily used to transport top-notch customers to view furniture which they would be purchasing in large quantities. About three times a year, the jets were scheduled to travel between three of our divisions strictly to transport employees back and forth for one-day meetings. I needed to go to our corporate headquarters for some training and a seat was available on one of the jets.

It was wonderful! If you have never traveled on a private corporate jet—it's a memorable experience. One nice benefit is you do not have to hassle with tickets. You don't have to check in and get seat assignments. Our jet seated seven plus two pilots. The inside was beautifully decorated and comfortable.

The jet was stocked with beverages, food, gum, mints, and snacks—all very compact. On the flight going up in the morning we were served (by one of the pilots) a lovely plate of fresh fruit, danish, muffins, juice, and coffee. When we arrived at the company's private hangar, we stepped right off the plane and someone was there waiting to take us each to our destination.

Our trip home welcomed us with trays of fresh deli meats and cheeses, fruits, and beverages. I felt totally pampered. Not only was the flight an experience, but I truly enjoyed seeing the corporate offices and learned many new things in my meetings that day. I came back feeling very satisfied and more knowledgeable about my job and the company as a whole. I also appreciated my boss for allowing me to be one of the lucky employees to travel via "corporate jet."

SURVIVAL TACTIC #12:

Take advantage of opportunities your company has to offer which will enhance your skills; broaden your knowledge of the company as a whole; provide personal satisfaction, a general feeling of well being; and enable you to meet face to face with those you normally only talk to over the phone.

Express to your manager your desire to grow and learn as much as possible about your position and the company. By doing this, you will be considered when opportunities do arise that meet your goals. In addition to expressing desire, you must also be specific as to the benefits you and your manager will derive as well as your company by supporting you.

When you have been given privileges or opportunities, be sure to follow-up with a thank you note to whomever was responsible. It's always a good idea to state what you learned from the experience and how you plan to use it in your job. This, of course, will open up doors for you in the future for similar opportunities.

13.
RED AS A BEET

There he stood. At least six feet tall, blue eyes, salt and pepper hair, a charming English accent, and a personality that all admired. He was a vice president in a multi-billion dollar corporation.

I had only been with the company for about 16 months as a Senior Secretary working for a director and wanted to move up in the organization to an Executive Secretary position. I had always heard wonderful things about this particular VP and thought how great it would be to work for him, but figured his secretary would never leave the company. Well, guess what? The day came and his secretary was leaving the organization. I applied for the position but felt I didn't have a chance—two secretaries who had been in his department for quite some time had applied as well as several others within the company.

There was one other major problem: Every time I would see this VP in the halls or cafeteria, I would blush—turn red as a beet. I would actually feel the color rising in my cheeks. I just felt intimated by his stature and position within the company. I remember thinking to myself: "How could I ever work for this person? I will turn red every time he calls me into his office!" But I wanted this promotion so badly and heard such great things about him being one of the best managers to work for, I realized I would have to get over this blushing nonsense.

I interviewed for the job and won out over many others. I blushed all during my interviews, and even on the day he made the job offer. But after that, no more blushing.

The 18 months I spent working for this individual were the best months of my entire career because he genuinely was a mentor to me.

SURVIVAL TACTIC #13:

Don't let the prestigious position of a manager intimidate you. Underneath all that can be a genuine, intelligent person who can teach you the business, has enough faith in you to delegate projects, and gives you responsibilities that will help you grow as a person and mature in your career.

If you ever are fortunate enough to have a boss who truly fulfills the role of business mentor, learn everything you can from that individual. Be thankful to be able to work with such a fine individual as they are far and few between.

14.
AEROBICS ANYONE?

We met three days a week during our lunch hour in the empty office space on the first floor of an office building. We would put on our best aerobic outfits, tennis shoes, and leg warmers. Boy, we looked good. Better yet, we felt terrific.

I'm sure you remember when aerobics just came into style. I worked out early every morning to an aerobic video tape at home. Many of the secretaries where I worked were trying to lose weight and improve their health. I suggested bringing in my tape three days a week and lead the group through the sessions. They loved the idea.

We had a pretty nice set up at this company. In our ladies rooms, we each had our own little locker where we could place our personal things to freshen up after the workouts. This was not only physically beneficial, but mentally helped us as we worked for a very intense international organization. The break at lunch released a lot of tension and pressure from the morning and replenished our energy for the afternoon. Plus we had fun. We ended up being admired by the management team for our dedication and commitment to getting healthy.

SURVIVAL TACTIC #14:

You may have outside interests that would contribute to the betterment of your company or to a particular group within your company. Be a leader. There are hundreds of followers, but very few leaders. Most people are great at participating as long as there is someone to tell them what to do. Few people want to or are committed to initiating activities in their organization. Being a leader does take organizational skills and motivation in order to get your troops together and keep them going. But the rewards are many.

Management loves leaders. When they need to promote someone, who do you think they look to? Those employees that have been leaders in their organization. Those individuals who are self-motivated. If you are serious about your career and moving up in your company, you need to be seen. You need to be known as an action person.

There are many ways you can do this besides starting an aerobics group. You can do things that specifically relate to the secretarial field such as starting a newsletter just for secretaries, organizing monthly brown bag lunches as an opportunity to network, initiating outside training brought in-house, or volunteering for committee work if your organization is conducting a special event.

15.
IT'S JUST BUSINESS

I was so excited. We had just moved to a small town in North Carolina and within two weeks I had what a small town considered to be a good job. Although it was very different from the Fortune 500 life I had been used to, this little 23-person computer company was to be my new challenge.

They had never had a true office manager. I went in determined to improve things and did, much to management's pleasure. However, unbeknownst to me, the company was having financial difficulty and by the end of six months they had to let me go. I was hurt since I had worked hard—put in many extra hours—and I really liked these people. I'll never forget the day my boss told me the bad news. That was the first time I had ever been "let go" from a job. We were in his office at the time. I could feel myself forcing back the tears.

I was fortunate in that months earlier I had interviewed at an advertising agency and left a good first impression. I contacted them immediately and, although they had no opening, were able to refer me to a manager with a large resort who was in need of an assistant. I left the computer company on a Friday and started working in the executive offices of the resort the following Monday.

SURVIVAL TACTIC #15:

1) Learn to leave out emotion—do not cry in front of management (if at all possible). As devastated as you might be by an event, hold back the tears until you get to your work station or a private area.

2) Learn to respond quickly. Get over the shock. Get over the tears and move forward. Life goes on. Start looking for a job immediately. Concentrate on aspects that you can control, rather than dwelling on what you can't control.

3) Learn to network with people outside your organization as well as always reflecting a professional image. You never know how much influence or what contacts someone may have. You never know when someone can help you in your career.

It's times like this that other contacts become important. As the result of my making a good impression with the executive at the ad agency, he gladly referred me and I ended up with another great job.

16.
GET ME OUT OF HERE

She and I hit it off great the first time we met. She was Vice President of Human Resources and was interviewing me for a position as Assistant to the CEO. It was also that very day I was offered the position right on the spot! With the money I wanted!

During this interview, she told me that the CEO was the most terrific person. And although I wasn't overly excited about where my work area was, which was smack in the center of a room surrounded by four offices so one felt like they were in a fish bowl, things could probably be rearranged.

It sounded like a good position. Assistant to the CEO—not too large of an organization. They had a corporate jet that flew the CEO back and forth from Nashville (where he presently lived) to Memphis (where he would be moving to shortly, or so I was told in the interview).

It was very strange that I never met or interviewed directly with the CEO prior to my starting day. I met him for the first time one week after I started the job. This hiring process was done through the female executive who was impressed with me and whom I felt I would get along with quite well. Plus, she raved about this executive and said I would enjoy working for him.

I trusted her judgment. Plus I was desperate for a job. We had just moved to Memphis a few months ago and I needed to go to work.

Within two weeks of starting my job, what I thought would be a great job, with a great boss, and a great little company, turned out to be a nightmare. Within two weeks I hated it. I wasn't at all crazy about the CEO. He had a very strange personality. Of course, any man who only uses an artist's drawing table for his desk is strange to me. The man did not even have a normal office. All he had was an art table with a telephone on it. No credenza. No file drawers. No rolodex. No visitor chairs. No personality!

I later found out he never had any intentions of moving to Memphis. He had a full time secretary in Nashville. Any communication and direction for me was done through the Human Resource Manager. If I recall during the two weeks I was there, the man directly talked to me one time.

Come to think of it, most of the people in the organization were strange. There was a loud-mouthed, cigar-smoking, rough spoken Vice President in an office about two feet away from my desk who insisted on keeping his door open all the time. He was a nice guy but had no class.

The other female Assistant who reported to the company President ran around in her stocking feet, had a very deep loud laugh, and reminded me of Attila the Hun. Needless to say, she and I did not hit it off very well. There was a glass door between her work area and mine which I would close to not be distracted by her loudness. When I wasn't looking, she'd come and open it. We would go back and forth with this little game several times a day.

The work itself was unchallenging, boring, and I hated it. Plain and simple. . .I was not a happy camper. I felt the job had been misrepresented to me by the employment agency as well as the company and two weeks later I left.

SURVIVAL TACTIC #16:

Always, always, always meet at least once and better yet, two or three times the person or persons whom you will be directly working for. I realize this was a unique situation but can happen to you. When you do meet this person, be sure to ask questions about the job, his expectations of the person who will fill the position, what his work style is, what are his goals in building a secretary/boss team, and how supportive he is of your continued growth and training.

Too many times, jobs and job responsibilities are misrepresented or perceived differently between a potential employee and employer when interviewing which later causes frustration and conflict. Remember, the company not only should want and like you, but you should also like the company. There should be mutual understanding and common goals for both parties.

It is also beneficial to go back a second time to talk with the manager. You get a different perspective of the people and see more of what goes on at the office. Some things to observe while waiting for your interview appointments are:

* the other employees
* how the employees interact with each other
* how they are dressed
* the office environment

Feel the atmosphere. Do people seem friendly? Do they seem to get along or are they rigid-looking? Is it crammed or is it a pleasant open environment?

Once inside the manager's office, glance at the surroundings. Is the office messy and unorganized? Notice little knickknacks, pictures, and decor. How does this person handle interruptions while you are interviewing? These things tell you a little bit about the person interviewing you.

If after you have accepted a job, you find yourself in a situation as I did where you are not happy getting up in the morning, not wanting to go to work, and dreading the day, get out of that job. Life is too short and your time is too precious to waste it working for someone you do not like or doing work that is unchallenging. Jump ship and find something you will love. If you love what you do and enjoy who you work with, you will do a great job and be successful at it.

I'm not saying to leave because of one thing. You need to weigh the situation. If only a few things are out of line, but you are pleased with everything else, then don't pack your bags. However, if you don't like your boss and co-workers, the work is unchallenging, you dislike the office environment and you are plain old miserable, then you might want to put on your walking shoes.

17.
CHARTS, CHARTS, AND MORE CHARTS

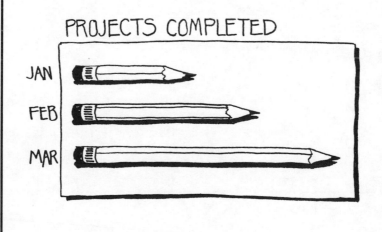

PROJECTS COMPLETED

Pie charts, line charts, organization charts, bar graphs, line graphs—you name it—he wanted it! Charts and graphs are very useful for presentations, reports, defining organizations, or to make a point. This one particular executive, though, I believed carried this a bit too far. Just about everything he wrote or presented had charts or graphs in them.

If I was working for him today, it wouldn't be so bad because of all the sophisticated software. But this was about eight years ago. Word processing was just coming into the work place. We were still using typewriters to create charts. There were no graphic programs or organization chart programs—you did it on the typewriter or spaced it out in word processing and then drew lines and boxes by hand. This made creating and editing charts extremely difficult and time consuming. Nonetheless, he wanted charts. He got charts.

SURVIVAL TACTIC #17:

When trying to present a point or state a position to your manager, learn to communicate to him in the manner or mode he understands. Get on the same wave length with your boss. In this instance, my boss's language was graphs and charts. He liked things presented to him visually.

So, when I wanted to make a point on a particular issue or initiate a new idea, I presented it in chart or graph form. I was talking a language he readily accepted. This was a very effective means of communicating with him.

Take time to learn your boss's preferred communication style. They all have one. Maybe he likes things short and to the point. Maybe he likes detailed lengthy summaries, background information, and supporting materials. Knowing this is especially useful when you are trying to "sell" an idea or want to stimulate change.

18.
THE PERFORMANCE REVIEW

I was really looking forward to this performance review. Even excited. Why this one in particular, when I had been through over 22 reviews in my career?

Because this was the first one I played a part in preparing myself with the management team six weeks prior to my review date. I made sure my manager and his executive staff, who I also assisted, knew everything I did in the past year.

I gave them a detailed five-page document outlining the many facets of my job, quantified certain routine tasks, and highlighted all the new responsibilities I had taken on as well as new skills I learned. This gave them a broader perspective of my job and exactly what it entailed. This document was also used as a basis of discussion during my review.

My boss was impressed with my taking the initiative of being actively involved in my review. It increased the level of respect and appreciation I received from him and his staff and resulted in a higher salary increase.

SURVIVAL TACTIC #18:

Prepare yourself and your boss for your review. Performance reviews are normally held annually. That means only once in 12 months will you have the opportunity for a raise. This is your time to bring out your strong points and toot your own horn.

Good managers have an idea of what you do and how you do it. But even really good managers do not know all the nitty gritty details you handle and they shouldn't except this one time. It would benefit you, providing you have been a top performer in the last 12 months, to prepare a document highlighting such things as: basic duties and tasks, special meetings and program preparation, new responsibilities, new skills learned as well as any equipment you have been trained to use.

Give this to your manager in a professionally prepared document format at least six weeks prior to your review, attach a cover letter indicating this is to assist him in preparing for your review and to be used as discussion material during the review process. Be sure to keep a copy for yourself!

By the way, a participant who learned this from me during a workshop told me she also used this document when a new boss came on board. It gave her new manager immediate insight to her job. Isn't that a great idea?

19.
ATHOL, MASSACHUSETTS!

I had accepted a position with a well-known, rather large company who was moving their offices from Massachusetts to Asheville, North Carolina where I was living at the time. I would have to spend two weeks at their headquarters in Athol, Massachusetts for cross-over training for my new position.

Two weeks did not sound too long to be away from my family. After all, I was told during the interview that the company limo would pick me up from the airport. I would be staying at a hotel where a group of other recruited employees were presently staying, and we would be training at the corporate offices. Sounds pretty good, doesn't it?

Little did I know the so-called corporate offices and manufacturing facility had been operating on a skeleton crew for the last 18 months due to a strike which never got resolved, eventually leading to the closing of the facility. The final decision to salvage what little was left of the division was to move the business to North Carolina—no union problems.

The offices were very old. They were dirty and dusty because there was no maintenance staff, nor were any cleaning people hired. In addition, the entire place would shut down within a few months once all final personnel and benefit issues had been handled. I, of course, brought suits to wear, thinking I was going to sophisticated corporate offices. Boy, was I surprised. The morale of the employees who had to train us was low because they were not going to have jobs in a few weeks. This in turn made them sometimes appear a bit unfriendly toward those of us from North Carolina.

Every night I went back to my cubicle of a room with dust and dirt all over my clothes and feeling half frozen because it was the middle of winter (and Athol is not the place to be in the middle of winter). Our so-called hotel was more like a hole-in-the-wall inn. It didn't have many rooms. Our group, therefore, was divided between two inns. I was told my group was staying in the nicer hotel. Can you imagine what the other was like?

The walls were so thin, you could almost hear the people breathing in the next room. I know you could hear them showering and brushing their teeth. There was one pay phone in the hall which was shared by 14 of us. We'd stand in line at night or anxiously wait at our door for someone to hang up so we could run up and call home. After all, that was the highlight of our entire day. There was a pool room in the hotel where the locals came at night to drink beer, play the jukebox, and keep us up most of the night. There was no place to eat and, if I remember correctly, there wasn't even a snack machine in the hall.

A few old cars were rented for us to take back and forth to the office each day. So much for the company limo! I guess they had to give that up when the strike started. The car I rode in generated very little heat. My driver (who happened to be my new boss) was from Athol and used to the bitter cold. He didn't feel it was necessary to put on much heat in the car. By the time I got to the office or back to the hotel, my feet were frozen.

It was a tough two weeks. I was in a physical environment which was depressing, being taught by people who were depressed, feeling frozen

69

most of the time, and isolated in a small town in the middle of nowhere.

As a group, we did make the best of it. We usually sat around at night talking about our experiences of the day and anxiously counted the days until we would go home. This was great therapy because we needed to keep our spirits up and our minds open to learn our new jobs.

I did survive the two weeks and flew home to work in brand new offices! No company limo, though.

SURVIVAL TACTIC #19:

1) Make the most of a bad situation. Learn from every experience whether it is a good or bad experience. You're not always going to have wonderful, easy-going situations. But if you can find one good thing in every situation—maybe just one lesson to learn—you will be a better person for it.

2) Bad experiences or stressful times tend to pull a group together, creating a feeling of team spirit. We definitely returned to North Carolina being a real team and put tremendous effort and energy into making our new offices a great place to work. Sometimes as a group, it is easier to laugh at things that otherwise might not be so funny if you were going through it alone. There is a special feeling you get from being a team player.

3) There are people who do have it harder than you or me. It's easy to forget this. I really felt sorry for those people who had put in so many years working at the facility in Athol. This was their life, their home. Many of them did not know what they were going to do and for that I felt sad. Many of them had never worked anywhere else.

4) I was thankful that in my previous 14 years of work, I had made several career changes. This made it easier for me to adapt when necessary, be flexible, and kept me marketable.

This is important to keep in mind in

our society today. Companies that were fat and healthy years ago are having to now cut costs and downsize. As the marketplace becomes more competitive and costs continue to rise, there will be more and more downsizing, acquisitions, and mergers occurring. Keep up your skills, keep yourself marketable, and always be prepared to deal with change.

It had been 18 years into my career. I had worked for about 10 different companies by now, in five different states. I had worked my way up. I had worked for some of the finest corporations and for some of the best executives. I started questioning where do I go from here? It was time to change careers, or so I thought. I had just moved to Memphis with my husband and two children. I searched for the right job with the right company and was unhappy over and over.

I finally applied for a position described in the paper as administrative assistant. When I went on the interview, it turned out they were looking for someone with administrative skills who they would teach to be a loan officer for a mortgage company. To keep my story short, I took the job, thinking maybe this was the change I was look- ing for. I spent five full days in training.

Two months into it, I hated it and went back to being a secretary. Which only lasted two more years before I finally started my own business.

SURVIVAL TACTIC #20:

There is a right time and a wrong time to make a career change. Sometimes you think you may want to do something else, but deep inside you aren't quite yet ready to make the change.

It's great to try new things because you never know when it will work out. But one thing for sure I have learned, your dream will become a reality at the right time. You can try to force it ahead of schedule, but then you usually pay for it later.

If you are at a crossroad in your career as a secretary or administrative assistant, start to plan and visualize where you would like to be in a few years. Career change does not happen over night, especially if you are thinking of leaving the field. It takes serious planning and months of preparation.

Sometimes, too, it may be that you just need a different job or need to add challenge to your present job. I know as a secretary sometimes your work can be unchallenging and even become boring. It's up to you to add creativity. It's up to you to think of ways to stimulate yourself and stay interested in the field.

21.
YOUR CONTRIBUTION TO QUALITY EXCELLENCE

There is not any one particular experience that stands out in my mind in relation to quality. That is because quality excellence was something I strived for all the years I worked as a secretary and administrative assistant. And is something I apply today in everything I do.

Quality excellence is a way of life. It doesn't happen just once in awhile. Striving for excellence should happen daily in everything you do. It is for everyone in every industry whether you make a product or provide a service.

Quality service. . .quality excellence. . .total quality management. . .these are the buzz terms of this decade. Although you may hear different terms and your company may have its own quality statement, they all say the same thing. They all fall under the concepts of quality.

The Japanese have an interesting word for this: Kaizan. It means continuous improvement. Quality isn't just something you achieve and then say to yourself "O.k., I can relax now"; it is continuous. It is the continual striving for excellence. It is setting goals for establishing excellence in what you do as a secretary or administrative assistant, reaching those goals, and then setting new ones while maintaining the quality on those already reached.

You are an integral player in helping your organization achieve quality. What part do you now play? If you haven't had some training on quality through your company, attend a seminar on the subject to learn the main concepts. Look at the back of this book for some reading references to help you.

SURVIVAL TACTIC #21:

In your role as secretary or administrative assistant, you are responsible for managing quality in your job. You manage quality through your skills and through your attitude.

If you think about the skills required to do your job, here are four easy concepts for you to remember.

1. *Do it right the first time.*

It is proven that 25 percent of non-manufacturing work is done over before it is done right. That is the work you and I do every day. For example:

* *if you haven't accurately proofread a letter and have to retype it.*

* *if you didn't check the number of copies of a document you want to print before sending it to queue and more letters print out than you need.*

* *if you don't take that extra few minutes to double check a report for accurate numbers and, therefore, have to do it over.*

Every time you have to do something over, you cost your company money. This cost comes in the form of time and/or use of supplies. How often have you gone to the copy machine and, because you were in a hurry, didn't check the settings and ended up with copies in legal size rather than letter or vice versa? You cost your company time because you have to stand there and redo the copying. You cost them money because of the paper that is wasted.

When you cost your company money it cuts into the profits. And affects you. It affects you and your benefits, pay increases, and perhaps opportunities to advance.

We all make mistakes and these instances will happen. But it should be your goal to "do it right the first time" and reduce that 25 percent re-work number.

2. *The Domino Effect*

An important aspect of managing quality is learning to prevent the domino effect from occurring. The domino effect means that when you don't take the time to do something accurately or completely and forward it to another person, it prevents that person from doing their job to the best of their ability. In turn, they might pass along work that is inaccurate or not complete. As a secretary or administrative assistant, everything you do affects something or someone.

Here is an example. You forget to pull some information that your manager needed to complete a report that is due to his manager today. Because of that, you made your manager late in getting his information to his manager, thus causing that manager a delay in his project. I bet you can think of many other similar situations.

To help prevent the domino effect, see beyond yourself and your own work area or department. Again, see how what you do affects someone or something else. Try to see the big picture.

You can ensure quality service happens by focusing on your skills and your attitude. Did you know it takes many skills to perform *one* task? To type a letter, you need the following skills: computer, proofreading, grammar and punctuation, communication, and sometimes organization.

If you have excellent skills, you will. . .

* increase productivity
* do the right thing
* do it the right way, the first time, on time
* be proud every time you initial your work
* be a strong link in your organization.

You know your attitude has a negative or positive impact on you and your quality of work. When you feel in a low mood, upset, or frustrated, it affects the way you treat people, your willingness to do the work right, and ability to recognize mistakes to learn from.

If you have a good attitude, you will. . .

* treat your internal and external customer better
* care about your job performance
* manage difficult situations and people more effectively
* see that your manager is taken care of
* meet the customer's expectations
* treat every customer with integrity, courtesy, and respect.

3. *The Customer*

Another important aspect of quality is the customer. Probably your first tendency when you hear the word customer is to think of that external person—someone outside the organization. However, you have internal customers that must be satisfied. That includes your boss, your boss's boss, other departments, and any people you might supervise. They, just as importantly, must be provided with what they need, when they need it, in the manner they need it.

4. *Managing Yourself*

Part of providing quality service is learning to manage yourself. It is understanding what is comfortable for you to do in your job and realizing those things that cause you to stretch. With that in mind, quality also is:

* stretching beyond your own comforts to meet the comforts and needs of those you serve
* changing a behavioral response to people and situations
* thinking of other's needs before your own
* going the extra mile
* and having an "I can do it" attitude.

If you will use the concepts mentioned here, you will be on your way to achieving excellence and helping your company reach their quality mission.*

---

*Joan M. Burge, CPS conducts a one-day workshop entitled *Your Contribution to Quality Service*™ which is designed specifically for secretaries, administrative assistants, and support staff. For more information, write: Office Dynamics, P. O. Box 120003, Norfolk, Virginia 23502 or call (804) 455-6866.

22.
CONCLUSION

In retrospect, being a secretary and administrative assistant or any other related title is very rewarding. It has its ups and downs, its great days and its bad days, its good bosses and bad bosses, just as many other careers. But it also offers rewards and opportunities. Many times, though, you will have to be the one to create those opportunities. You will have to be the one to take a frustrating or embarrassing experience and make it interesting or treat it as a learning experience.

This field prepares you for other areas you may want to pursue in the future such as customer service, public relations, marketing, management positions, sales, financial work, and many other careers. It provides you with many skills and experiences that would benefit you if the day should come you want to start your own business. They helped me!

References on Quality

Albrecht, Karl & Zemke, Ron. *Service America: Doing Business in the New Economy*. Homewood, IL: Dow Jones-Irwin, 1985.

Crosby, Philip B. *Quality is Free*. New York: McGraw Hill Book Company, 1979.

Kilman, Ralph H. *Beyond the Quick Fix*. San Francisco: Jossey-Bass Inc., Publishers, 1984.

Kolbe, Kathy. *The Conative Connection: Uncovering the Link Between Who You Are and How You Perform*. Reading, MA: Addison Wesley Publishing Co., 1990.

Peters, Tom. *Thriving on Chaos*. New York: Knopf, 1987.

Scherkenbach, W.W. *The Deming Route to Quality and Productivity*. Washington, DC: Ceep Press Books, 1986..

Scholtes, Peter R. *The Team Handbook*. Madison, WI: Joiner Associates, 1988.

More About Joan M. Burge, CPS:

Photo by Billy Ross

Joan Burge is president and founder of Office Dynamics, a consulting and training firm specializing in developing management support and secretarial personnel. She is the author of the Star Achievement™ Series, a four-part training program designed specifically for secretaries and management support personnel, and author of the Advanced Star Achievement™ Series. Joan is also president and founder of The Star Achievers™ organization, a unique organization for executive assistants and executive secretaries reporting to presidents, managing partners, and CEOs of reputable firms.

She is a Certified Professional Secretary with over 20 years of experience in a variety of industries ranging in size from small personal businesses to Fortune 500 companies. She is a talented and motivated speaker, and has addressed hundreds of secretaries and administrative assistants throughout the United States.

Mrs. Burge is available for on-site seminars and consultation, guest speaking, and conducting of personality assessments. Write or call: Joan M. Burge, CPS, Office Dynamics, Post Office Box 120003, Norfolk, Virginia 23502. (804) 455-6866